Self Love: A Spiritual Guide to find the Inner You

How to Eliminate Negative Thoughts, Transform Your Mindset into Positive Thinking and Find Your Inner Peace incl. Self Love Journal

Kate A. Bailey

Table of Contents

SCAN QR CODE AND GET AUDIO BOOK

FOR FREE!

To my dear readers,

We are thankful that you decided to buy this book. As special gift we can offer you the audio book for free. Just scan the QR code and download for free on Audible:

Please scan with your mobile phone:

*Just possible for new Audible customers.

Introduction

Do you still feel confused by your thoughts? Do you battle the tasks you have to complete every week with tension or anxiety? Would you like to stop thinking about life in general? From time to time, we all experience negative thinking. But if you ever feel stressed, you can analyse closely what you are thinking and how your thinking affects your mental well-being.

This inner monologue is a natural part of your mind. It's still there night and day and reminds you of the food you need to choose, shame you for skipping, on your sister's birthday or are worried about the latest news (like politics, the environment, or the current state of the economy). These thoughts constitute the background noise of your life, even though your presence may not always be known. Just take a second and be careful of your feelings. Try to stop them. Try to stop them. It's tough. You can see how they continue to stream one by one, unbidden and sometimes unwanted. Any of your ideas are random and unnecessary.

"It's my arm that itches." "It looks like it will rain." "Where have I been placing my keys?" Many of our emotions are distracting and pessimistic, on the other hand. "The man's a shit." "This project I messed up." "What I said to Mom, I feel so bad." If they're negative, neutral, or optimistic, these thoughts embarrass our minds, just like when you have too many things, you can embarrass your house. Unfortunately, it is not so easy to clear your mental disorder as to remove a possession. You can't "throw away" a thought and wait until it's gone. In reality, like a never-ending Whack-a-Mole game, your negative thoughts will come back when you throw them down.

Why Do We Think Of Negative Ideas?

Now, visualise your mind as a wholly organised house – a home free of foreign, draining, and pointless objects that disturb you. What if you can only surround yourself with thoughts that elevate, encourage, and ease you? Consider your mind for a moment as a peaceful cloudless sky, and you have the power to choose what is in it. Why do we think so much, with so little filter, if this bright mental sky is so ideal that we sort constructive and necessary thinking out of the unnecessary and the random? There are about 100 billion neurons in your brain and another billion in your spinal cord. The total number of interactions between neurons – processing cells – is estimated at 100 trillion synapses. Our healthy brains actively process and analyse all kinds of interactions in the form of thoughts.

Thoughts shape what we see as truth. We can control our thoughts and guide them, but it also feels like our thoughts have minds of themselves; we control them and how we feel. To solve issues and make decisions, thinking is essential. Still, the mind wanders like a wild monkey between positive mental efforts and draws you through the brambles of rumination and negative thinking. Your daily internal dialogue, here and now, distracts you from what is going on around you. It leads you to miss meaningful experiences and sabotage the joy of today. We believe that we have to think more or more to "figure out" why we aren't as satisfied or accomplished as we would like to be. We strive to identify possessions, people, and experiences that can quench our desires and alleviate our misfortunes.

The more we reflect on our despair, the more we become depressed. Our thoughts make us nervous, empty, and restless as we search for answers into the future or the past. Indeed, almost every negative thought you have concerns the past or the future. It is usual to be stuck in a looping cycle of distressing ideas or worrying thoughts, even when desperate to avoid the endless tape playing in your head. You battle not only with your emotions but also with your unwillingness to be free.

The more you continue to loop the negative emotions, the worse you feel. It's almost like two of you

– the thinker and the judge, the person who thinks and who knows you think about them and how poor they are. This complex thinking/judging contains painful emotions. The more afraid, guilty, regrettable thinking we have, the more nervous, anxious, and angry we feel. Often our feelings paralyse us with negative feelings, and they deprive us of inner peace and satisfaction. While our feelings are the culprit for so much suffering, we believe nothing is to be done about it.

You can't interrupt your thoughts. You can't shut your brain off at will or get rid of the talk and related emotions that keep you from thoroughly enjoying life. Often, we have a spontaneous inner calm and quiet moments. However, we most frequently attempt to quench our mental discourses by using too much food, alcohol, narcotics, job, sex, or exercise. However, these are temporary remedies for silencing noise and alleviating pain. Our minds are back to it soon enough, and the cycle continues. Are we still doomed to be victims of our "monkey minds?"

Do we have to continuously fight our thoughts and allow them to make us feel worried, sorry, and anxious? Is there a way to have a simple, pain-free mind? You may not always be able to keep your mind clear of turmoil, but you can have a profound influence on your thinking to increase your overall quality of life and happiness. A thought may look automatic and uncontrollable, but many of our thinking habits are usual and, well, thoughtless. Although it seems like you and your thinking are inseparable, you have a "conscious self" that can step in and control your thinking.

You regulate your emotions far more than you realise. If you understand how to handle your mind, open the door to the immensity of imagination, inspiration, and brilliance behind the untouched mind. You will inspire your thoughts and have more room in your mind to experience inner peace and happiness through different practices of consciousness and realistic habits. You will have the clarity to prioritise the essential thing in your life, the things that no longer serve your purposes, and how you want to live every day.

Self Emotional

There are thousands of people who, when they were up, were sexually abused, ignored, or smothered by their parents or other caretakers. Many of these people don't know they have been abused or neglected, and they are still living with countless challenges because they don't get the support they need. People who internalise violence show self-destruction, depression, suicidal thoughts, passivity, retraction (avoidance of social contacts), timidity, and poor connection with others.

They may have low self-esteem and feel guilty and sorrowful, or they may be depressed, lonely, rejected, or resigned. Considered unworthy and the environment hostile, many people do not want to attempt new tasks, learn new skills, or take risks. People outsourcing violence could be erratic and aggressive, their actions being marked not by adherence to societal standards but by impulsive action. They are also nervous, violent, and hostile. They are always afraid and are always alert and willing to strike.

Many end up abusing people, sometimes in the same way that they were abused. A deficiently defined sense of oneself and a distorted view of oneself are the keys to all these symptoms and habits centred on parental negative messages and care. If adult survivors do not deal with these underlying problems, they will thwart their rehabilitation efforts. If you were a victim of emotional abuse or childhood neglect, this book shows you just what it takes to cure your self-image and self-esteem of the harm you suffer.

Healing Your Emotional Self will lead you step by step in a creative and psychologically sound program. It utilises the mirror as a metaphor, a tool of cure, and a psychologically sound one because it incorporates my long years of experience dealing with persons whose psychological principles have been emotionally misused.

Chapter 1

Perfectionism is the highest order of self-abuse.
—ANN SCHAEF WILSON.

I stop looking as much as I can in the mirror. When I look, my imperfections are all I see – my long nose, my twinkled teeth, my little breasts. I'm attracted to other people, but I don't see it.
—Kristin, twenty-six years old.

I'm what you'd call a perfectionist, particularly in my work. It takes me twice as long as others do things because I've got to go over it twice to make sure I haven't made any mistakes. My boss complains that I'm too late, but I'd prefer him to say that than to find him an error. That would ruin me. It would destroy me.
—Elliot, thirty-one years old.

In my mind, there is a voice continuously chastising me with "Why did you do that?" "Why have you said that?" The critique is unfailing. Nothing I've ever done is right. I'm never good enough. I'm never good enough. Often I feel like yelling—shut up! Let me alone! Please leave me alone!

—Teresa, forty-three years old.

I don't know what it's going to take to feel good about myself at last. I continue to think I need to do more, be a better person, and then I like myself. Some people are fascinated with how much I've accomplished in my life, but how much I do doesn't seem to matter; I'm never good enough for me.

—Charles, fifty-five years old.

Do you relate these people to anyone? Have you had a hard time looking in the mirror and what you see you never like? Do you not find yourself satisfied, no matter how much you make yourself a better person, regardless of the amount of work you do on your body? Are you still finding fault with yourself? Are you a perfectionist? Are you troubled by an internal critic that constantly annoys you or considers everything you do wrong? Or are you like Charles, who thinks that your achievements are the way to feel good about yourself—but how much you accomplish is never enough? Many of us concentrate on changing our bodies and making ourselves more desirable.

Yet many don't like who they see in the mirror with all the time and money they spend on nutrition, exercise, clothing, and cosmetic operations. Everything must always be modified or strengthened. People who are self-conscious about their appearance often criticise other aspects of their lives. They prefer to concentrate on their shortcomings instead of their assets, and they rarely appreciate their success, whether at work, at school, or in relationships. You punish yourself mercilessly if you make a mistake. There is nothing wrong with trying to better you; everyone has self-critical thoughts from time to time. But certain people have such poor self-esteem that they are never satisfied with their success, image, or performance. They have a persistent critique that relentlessly breaks them down and steals their happiness from the target they may momentarily feel. The following questionnaire helps you to decide whether you have low self-esteem and an unhealthy inner critical.

Quest: To "SELF" Review. Query.

1. Are you suffering from fear or distrust?

2. Do you concentrate more on what you do wrong or fail than on what you do right or good?

3. Do you feel less or less good than most, because of what you do or what you look like you're not perfect?

4. Do you think you have to do more, be more or offer more to win other people's love and respect?

5. Are you conscious that you have a vital inner voice that always alerts you that something was wrong?

6. Do you criticise your results constantly – at work, at school, in sports?

7. Are you critical of how you interact?

8. In life, in your work, in your relationships, do you feel like a failure?

9. Do you worry about success or happiness?

10. Are you worried you wouldn't like youself if people knew you real?

11. Are you ever overcome with embarrassment and guilt because you feel exposed, mocked, or ridiculed?

12. Compare yourself continuously to others and fall short?

13. Are you aware of yourself or embarrassed by the way you look?

14. Do you have an eating disorder – compulsive excessive eating, bingeing and cleansing, common diet, hunger or anorexia?

15. Do you have to drink alcohol or take other drugs to feel better or less aware of yourself in social situations?

16. Don't you care about yourself very well with bad diets, too little sleep or exercise?

17. Did you ever consciously injure yourself that is, cut yourself off?

If you responded yes to more than five of these questions, you'll benefit from the extra help in this book to boost your self-esteem, relax your inner critic, heal your shame, and begin to find true joy and pride in your accomplishments. Even if you replied only yes to one of these questions, this book will support you, since one of these feelings is not normal or safe. In moments of self doubt, you have been born with an innate sense of goodness, courage and knowledge. Unfortunately, this inner sense may have lost you because of the way you were raised and the messages you got.

Identified Self-Esteem

Let's start by identifying and distinguishing self-esteem from self-image and self-conception. Self-esteem is how you feel like an individual – your overall judgment. Depending on how much you like or approve of yourself, your self-esteem can be high or low. If you have high self-esteem, your personality is fully appreciated. This means that both your positive and your so-called negative qualities are appropriate for who you are. It can be concluded that you have admiration for yourself, self-love, and self-worth feelings. You don't have to please anyone because you know you're worth it already. If you can't tell if your self-esteem is high, ask yourself, "I think I'm a lovely one?" "I think I'm worthwhile, do I?"

Our self-worth emotions are at the heart of our personality. For our psychological well-being, nothing is so critical. The degree of confidence impacts pretty much every part of our lives. It influences how we view ourselves and how people perceive us and then treat us. This impacts our life decisions, from our professions on which we become friends or become romantic. It affects how we get along with others and how effective we are in using our skills. It affects our ability to function when things have to be modified and when we are able to be imaginative. It affects our stability, even though we are supporters or leaders. It is only reasonable that the degree of self-esteem, our general feeling, may also influence our ability to shape interpersonal relationships.

Many people use the words self-esteem and self-conception interchangeably, but in fact, these concepts mean differently. Our self-image is the collection of values or images we have about ourselves. Our self-esteem is the measure of how much we like and how much we accept our conception.

Another way of thinking is how much respect you have for yourself and how you see yourself. Another way of differentiating between self-esteem and self-image is to see self-esteem as something to offer you. Self-image is usually focused on how you imagine others view you. (This is why it's called "self-esteem".) Our self-image consists of a wide range of photographs and convictions. Some are obvious and easily verifiable ("I'm a woman," "I'm a therapist," for instance). But there are other less concrete facets of the self (e.g., "I am smart," "I am competent") as well.

Your Real Cause Or Your Negative Self-Image

Your low self-esteem or negative self-image is possibly caused mainly by your childhood. Despite what befell you, your parent (or individuals who received you) essentially affected how you feel about yourself. Hostile parenting and messages will profoundly influence our self-image and self-esteem. This applies in particular to survivors of sexual violence, neglect, or childhood smothering. Inadequate, dysfunctional parenting may affect the formation, self-conception, and self-esteem of a child. Research indicates that the most significant element in assessing a child's self-esteem is the childhood style of his or her parents in the first three or four years of the child's existence.

When parents love, encourage, and are fair-minded and advocate reasonable discipline and set appropriate boundaries, their children are optimistic, self-monitoring, self-realised. But parents who are critical, neglectful and unreasonable with their punishment and judgement limits, their children will not be safe and they will feel low self-appreciation. I was struck by his dark good looks when I first saw Matthew. He looked like a younger, larger exotic Tom Cruise with chiselled features, broad, dark, almond-shaped eyes, and straight dark hair. I expected him to talk to me with confidence because he was so strikingly good-looking, and instead, he spoke in a reticent, almost appropriate manner.

When he explained to me why he was on therapy, I found himself somewhat uncertain. While he was a smart, talented and beautiful young man, he was tormented by self-doubt and critical of himself. Why would a young man feel so badly about himself with so much going for him? When Matthew told me his life story, I found his dad never satisfied him. It never was enough, regardless of what Matthew did. When he was on the honorary scene in school, he told me about it and was excited to tell his father. Instead of congratulating and proudly Matthew, his father said to him that he wanted to get a job after school because school was too austere for him. So Matthew did as suggested by his father. But neither did this seem to impress him.

Instead, his dad complained that the yard work wasn't enough and that he had to leave his job. "You work so you can make money to waste on girls," his dad criticised, not realising somehow that he was the one who predicted Matthew's first job. Matthew was very musically interested and a very talented piano player. But his dad wasn't pleased with his lessons. "You're too effeminate now," he scoffed. "Why are you not going out in school for sports as I did?" As Matthew followed the advice of his father and tried the track team, his father complained: "It's just not as prestigious as playing football or basketball. Why don't you try one of the teams?" Since his father was never proud of him and his achievements never acknowledged, Matthew got brutal with himself. He became rather self-critical; he noticed something wrong about it, no matter what he achieved.

If anyone tried to compliment him, he would have loved them with comments like "Wow, everyone could," "Yeah, but you would have seen how I messed up yesterday." Matthew's father had made him aware of himself and afraid of not recognising Matthew and never being happy. Many parents weaken their children's self-esteem and build in them some "self anxiety" by treating them in the form of a lack of warmth and affection, recognition, appreciation, and admiration and an unrealistic expectation, dominion, indifference, degradation, and alienation.

"Inner criticism" defined.

Another element in developing low self-esteem is solid internal critic, which usually goes hand in hand with low self-esteem. Your inner criticism is created by the normal phase of socialisation experienced by any child. Parents teach their children what actions are appropriate, immoral, harmful, or morally incorrect. Most parents love the former and discourage the latter. Children realise that their parents are a source of physical and emotional nourishment, either consciously or unconsciously.

So their parental acceptance feels like a matter of life or death. When they are scolded or spread, they often feel very acutely that parental approval has been withdrawn, and it brings with it the horrific possibility of losing all protection.

All children keep conscious and unconscious memories of those moments when they feel bad or wrong because of the lack of acceptance from their parents. This is the beginning of the inner critic. (I use "he" to refer to the inner critic because many people, including women, believe that their inner critics are male. Feel free to replace "she" if it sounds better for you.) Even as an adult, some of you still think you're "wrong" if someone gets upset at you or if you make a mistake. Your internal critique's voice is the voice of a disapproving parent, the punitive voice that forbids your childhood conduct. If your early experiences are mild and proper, your adult critic will rarely target you. Still, if you have had obvious signals about your childhood "badness" or "wrongness," your adult critic can always and ferociously attack you.

Identified Emotional Abuse And Neglect

Abuse is an extreme term mentally. It typically means the abuser's intention or even malice. But a parent who finds joy in abusing and neglecting their children do so deliberately. Most of them are just copying how they were handled as a child – doing what was done to their children. Many do not know how dangerous they are to their children. Few do so out of malice – an deliberate attempt to injure their children. Low self-esteem is typically not taught by the parents' conscious or intentional efforts in children. And those parents who emotionally assault, neglect, or smother their children do not usually understand the enormous power they have to shape the sense of themselves of their children.

If we use the terms emotional violence, we need to be very precise. A child's emotional abuse is a behavioural trend, which means it happens continuously over time. Emotional violence is not perceived to be occasionally negative behaviour or behaviour. Also, the best of the parents had opportunities where they briefly lost their roles and told their children hurtful things, refused to give them their attention, or were frightened of their behaviour.

Each parent treats its children somehow, but passionately cruel parents habitually handle their children in some or all forms. Emotional abuse is a behaviour pattern that attacks the dynamic growth and self-worth of the infant. Since emotional abuse affects the feeling of the child, the victim becomes incapable of love and affection. Emotional violence can include both parent and caregiver behaviours and omissions and can trigger severe behavioural, cognitive, emotional, or childhood mental illnesses. This type of abuse has:

- Oral harassment (including perpetual blame, mocking, accusing, demeaning, abusive, eliminating, and inappropriate teasing).

- Put unfair or unrealistic demands on a child beyond its ability.

- To be overly regulated.

- Smothering a child emotionally (including being overprotective or unwilling to allow the child to create a separate life from her parents).

- Rejecting or leaving a child emotionally (including being cold and unresponsive and withholding love).

Neglect is a term that is much more misunderstood and can manifest physically and emotionally. Failure to provide for the child's basic physical needs (food, water, shelter, hygiene) and emotional, social, environmental, and medical needs requires physical failure of the parent or primary caregiver. Furthermore, it does not have sufficient supervision. Emotional neglect does not provide the requisite care and constructive support for the emotional and psychological growth and development of a child – providing little to no affection, support, or direction. This includes not considering a child's need for recognition, appreciation, and emotional support (non-interest in a child's emotions, activities, and problems). The following questionnaire will help you understand emotional abuse and neglect and decide whether you were a child.

Questionnaire: Would you have been emotional, neglected, or mothered in childhood?

1. Were you ever blamed for doing the wrong things or doing the bad thing?

   ....

   ....

   ....

2. Have you got the feeling that your parents would never approve of you, no matter what you did?

   ....

   ....

   ....

3. Were you disciplined or punished because, in any way, you did things?

   ....

   ....

   ....

4. Did your parents call you names that were insulting?

    ....
    ....
    ....

5. Have your parents belittle you, or have they made you a target of cruel or sadistic jokes?

    ....
    ....
    ....

6. Did your parents neglect your physical needs, for example, by the lack of sufficient clothing in the winter, such as a warm coat?

    ....
    ....
    ....

7. Were your parents so concerned or busy with their own needs or concerns that they took no time to be with you?

    ....
    ....
    ....

8. Were you deprived of physical nutrition (for instance, if you were upset or comforted) or affection as a child?

....

....

....

9. As a kid, was one of your two parents far away or aloof to you?

....

....

....

10. Have an alcohol habit, a drug or a gambling addiction, or some other addiction caused either or both of your parents to neglect you?

....

....

....

11. Have you ever been abandoned (you were never sent to live as punishment with anyone else or because a parent was ill or couldn't care for you)?

....
....
....

12. Has either or both parents been excessively protecting or overly afraid that you will suffer harm (for example, you could not engage in sports or regular childhood activities because you are scared of being hurt)?

....
....
....

13. Did one of your parents exclude you from others or fail to offer you friends or go to other kindergartens?

....
....
....

14. Are you too possessive of one or both of your parents (which is, did he or she seem jealous if you paid attention to someone else or had a friend or romantic partner)?

....

....

....

15. Did either or both parents treat you as a trustee, or have you sought emotional comfort?

....

....

....

These questions explain different kinds of emotional violence and neglect. If you responded yes to all of questions 1 to 5, your verbal abuse or unrealistic expectations emotionally abused you. You were ignored or abandoned as an infant when you answered yes to questions 6 to 12. If you answered yes to questions 13 to 16, you had emotional smothering or emotional incest.

Psychological Violence

While most emotional abuse and neglect on the part of a parent is unintentional, parents often intentionally harm their weapons. Psychological maltreatment is a phrase used by clinicians in describing an adult's deliberate assault on the growth of children's self-and social skills – a psychologically dangerous trend. There are sometimes five main types of conduct under the definition of emotional abuse:

- Rejection – compartments that communicate or constitute abandonment of the infant, such as refusal of affection.

- Isolation – preventing children from taking part in usual social interaction opportunities.

- Terrorisation – threatening a child with extreme or sinister punishment or an atmosphere of fear or danger.

- Ignoring the fact that the caregiver is inaccessible to the child and cannot react to the child's actions.

- Corrupt – care giving behaviour promotes the development of false social ideals, strengthening antisocial or deviant behavioural behaviours such as violence, crime, or substance misuse.

The Role Of Shame In Creating Low Self-Confidence And Perfection

Shame is a deep feeling in us that we are exposed and worthless. We want to cover when we are shamed. We hang our heads, shoulder our shoulders, and turn inward as if we were trying to make ourselves invisible.

Emotional abuse and neglect are very disgraceful experiences, and victims of it feel ashamed and abused. Moreover, most of the kids blame their parents for treating them, believing somewhat they should be handled in such a way that they think, "If I had just thought of my mother, she wouldn't have shouted at me in front of my peers."

This is an effort to reclaim a sense of control. It is more tolerable than the reality of utter helplessness to blame yourself and believe that you should have done differently or avoided an accident. Children brought up by parents who always scolded, reprimanded, or spanked them if they did the slightest wrong grow up feeling their own being wrong – not just their behaviour.

Some people battle guilt by seeking excellence. This is a way to compensate for a deficiency underlying meaning. The argument (even if subconscious) goes like this: "If I can get great, I'm never going to be shamed again." Naturally, this quest for perfection is doomed to fail. As the person who suffers from shame does not already feel good enough, nothing that he or she does will ever be considered good enough. Thus, if you continue to seek perfection in yourself, your self-esteem will be constantly frustrated and constantly damaged.

How Your Sense Of Self Affects Emotional Abuse And Neglect

So far, I have used several terms to describe various aspects of the self, including self-image, self-conception, and self-esteem. But the definition of self has not been described to date. There are several meanings, but we will describe it as your inner centre for our purposes. You have the sense of yourself as a separate person—the sense in which your needs and feelings disappear and others begin. There is another word "self" that needs to be defined: a sense of self. It's your inner consciousness of who you are and how you fit into the universe.

The ideal is called a "coherent sense of self", which has an inner sense of solidarity. You perceive yourself as an individual who has a place in the world, is entitled to speak, is able to influence and engage in what happens to you. Unfortunately, people that have been abused or ignored throughout their youth have a feeling of themselves, which is also defined by emotions that are nothing but inspiring. Rather, they feel powerless, shameless, angry, frightened, and guilty, leading to insecure feelings. We don't necessarily have contact with ourselves unless something happens that makes us pay attention to it. If someone disregards or ignores your achievements, your attention will turn inward.

You start to ask whether you are worthy or lovable. The other way around may also be accurate. You might turn inward to congratulate yourself if someone praises you. Being self-conscious means that for whatever reason, you are worried about how you do or how you meet others. This self-assessment can become obsessive and can either cause you to feel inhibited or shown to others. However, the desire to be your true self interferes with self-awareness.

When other people (particularly our parents) neglect or deny us, we sometimes start worrying about what we have done to warrant this reaction. This starts at an early age. Children are self-centred – that means they take it all about them, and therefore they must be the source of reactions from others – and they appear to blame themselves for the way others treat them. When we get older, we become self-aware, feeding our self-awareness with many self-deprecating assumptions. You had to be educated in an atmosphere where constructive psychological nourishment was available to create a healthy sense of self. The following are positive psychological nourishments:

- **Empathic answers.** When we say that someone has the ability to sympathise, we usually mean that they can hear and react to someone without getting picked up, or lost in their own view. She should put herself in the role of the other person – imagine how the other person feels. Unfortunately, many parents are so focused on themselves that they have no time or space for other people's needs or thoughts – even their own children. A traditional no empathic response from a parent will lead to a baby's impatience when a parent tries to prepare for parties. An empathic parent can take a deep breath, lovingly take her child up and remember that the baby can't help her. She's going to speak to the child sweetly and worry for him while she changes his diaper. A non-empathic parent can blame the child for a delay, treat the child roughly, and express disagreement to him.

- **Having confirmed your perceptions.** A primary way to encourage a positive sense of self is for parents to affirm the perspective of a child, for example, if a parent decides that something is triste if the child feels sad. This type of affirmation normally gives the child a feeling of being okay. She thinks that with her emotions she is "on goal", and probably also feels less alone in the world. If the parent tells the child, however, that a sad thing really is happy, the child can suddenly feel out of control or something is wrong. She'll probably also feel very lonely.

- **Having valued your individuality.** When respect for the uniqueness of a child as an individual, he learns to tolerate differences in himself and others. He discovers that discovering differences and dealing with them constructively is interesting. Unfortunately, in many families, different interests are not considered common for people in the same family. Instead, it is assumed that if a child has another choice or disagreement it tries to dominate its guardians or participates in a power fight. Some are also disciplined or accused of differing from others. In the mind of the boy, this is translated into the message "I am evil." On the other hand, if the individual interests of a child are respected, he continues to feel, "I'm okay." This, in turn, encourages a feeling of self that is worthy and cherished.

Chapter 2

As A Mirror, The Body

Self-disdain Never Inspires Lasting Change

Your feel and care for your body are integral aspects of your overall sense of self-worth and self-esteem. All the work you do in this book will help increase your self-esteem, but we will concentrate in this chapter on your body image. We will start by encouraging you to become more conscious of your body image and where your ideas came from. Then in the book, we will concentrate on how you can boost your body image lastingly and meaningfully.

Body image is your opinion or impression of your physical appearance – how it appears and what you think it looks like for others. For certain people, a negative body image is a source of low self-esteem, while for others low self-esteem comes first, and consequently the negative body image.

Our bodies also represent our feelings. What does your body say? How does your overall sense of self-worth reflect it? Is your body saying, "I'm so nice about me," or is it saying, "I'm so crappy about myself?"

Besides the way you feel, your body reflects several other things, including:

- How comfortable in the world do you feel?

- Your emotional or physical health level.

- How much you have been cared for as a child physically and emotionally.

- Your parents' messages on self-care.

- Texts from your parents (and others) about your body's feelings.

The sad truth is that you do not appreciate even though you have an almost perfect body. This is particularly true if you were neglected or abused as a child emotionally. You can tend to look for the slightest shortcoming and concentrate on your imperfections so much that they seem to overlook all your other good qualities. Some people do this to the point of developing a condition called body dysmorphic disorder, or BDD.

Many teenagers are continually worried about their weight and appearance, but some are concerned with a particular defect or perceived defect. This was the case for Kimberly, sixteen years old. Kimberly was persuaded her chin was too high. She looked regularly in the mirror and examined her chin from different angles and she obsessed with the best hair-style. She didn't trust them when others tried to reassure her that her chin looked okay. Actually, she persuaded her parents to send her to a plastic surgeon to fix the issue. When her parents declined to let her do the operation, she was furious and refused to go to school again. Her conduct has rightly indicated to her parents that it is more than the traditional adolescent fascination with looks. Kimberly required therapeutic treatment.

Avoiders And Obsessors

People with self-esteem, physical images and self-criticism appear to fall into two main groups – Obsessors and Avoiders – and are very diverse in dealing with the mirror.

Obsessors are concerned with the way they look and sometimes, if not always, look into the mirror. They check their facial tissues, hair and teeth and obsess about every part of the body that they feel is too fat, too thin, too long, or too crazy. When they get dressed, they obsess about whether a garment looks nice and sometimes look at the mirror the whole day to see whether it looks okay.

The avoider will quickly check the mirror when dressed during the day to make sure their hair or make-up is OK. Otherwise, they seldom look in the mirror. Many avoiders check inside the mirror without looking really – just a brief look to ensure that their clothes fit or their lipstick is not smeared – but avoid looking too closely. This fear of the mirror may be due to a fundamental rejection of their appearance. It is hard for them to look at themselves for this reason. Others feel so hideous on the inside they just see hideousness when they look inside the mirror – no matter how attractive it is.

Do You Carefully Judge Yourself?

The lousy picture of most people represents the fact that something happened during their childhood to erode their faith. Sadly, we all learn that beautiful people are often more dignified from a young age (for example, recent research shows that parents treat their attractive children better than their unattractive children). And in our specific social circle, we are all taught only what is considered beautiful

This training starts very early when outsiders give the most attention to the slimmest babies and children. Slowly, when children grow up, they are handled a certain way, depending on the sweetness, the wear of clothing, and the colour of the skin. Studies showed that beautiful children are more self-confident and have higher self-esteem than children considered less attractive.

If adults were pleased to smile and tell you what a sweet thing you were, how nice or how handy you were when you grew up, you probably felt really well about your body and your look. When, though, inessential adults say things like, "My, she's a fat person, isn't she?" Or, you probably didn't feel so good about your appearance (implying that he doesn't look like his attractive mother).

Acceptance And Rejection By Peers

Acceptance by peers is extremely critical for children and teenagers. If you are accepted, you have a high level of self-esteem, while those with refusal, teasing, or indifference appears to have lower self-esteem.

Calling a name is especially damaging to children and can have a negative impact on their body image. Names like "Fatso" may last a lifetime with a person like Hank: "When you have named yourself a "nerd" or a "fag" most of your babies, it is very difficult to think of yourself as sexually attractive to women.

Any time I think I even ask a kid, those words always ring in my ears." Rejection or indifference from the opposite sex can be especially damaging to a person's physics and maybe the beginning of a young person who believes he or she is unattractive or desirable, as she did with Ellen:

"Boys just never listened to me in school. I was taller than anyone, and my parents weren't able to afford to purchase my clothes in a specialty store and usually were either too short or too long. I never gave up trying to get their attention when I was in junior high school."

Chapter 3

Discover Your True Work

My friend Day is an impermanent artist on Earth. With a little ket in hand, he goes out every morning to gather seedpods, flowers, leaves, and any other elements of beauty that nature gives him that day. He then goes down the river near his house and cleans the remnants of yesterday's production from the ground using his hand to brush old art to make a new white dirt canvas. He painstakingly, lovingly, tenderly designs the colourful arrangement of hues, shapes, and shapes of his collected pieces. The art he produces is very similar to the mandalas built by Buddhist monks.

The results of his work are so astounding, so beautifully designed that when I see photographs of his Morning Altars, I sometimes weep or cry out loudly.

Like my friend Day, who will make a new work of art every morning, you too are an artist, whether you know it or not. Your canvas is your own life. Your art is how you show yourself – intentionally and passionately – nothing that you do. If we live our life from this viewpoint, we will find inspiration, rhythm, connection, synchronicity, and magic, and then the vibration of our inner energy increases like nothing else can.

Living your life as an artist is an idea contrary to the prevailing paradigm of the Western world, which uses our rational minds and our sheer will to 'conquer' obstacles on the way, to influence the results of each situation, and to achieve or 'win' the game of life. The quest for "more" is the background to this way of life. As our world in the so-called information age is becoming faster and more technologically based, we move at an agitated pace, always wanting more information at our fingertips, more Facebook friends or Instagram loves, and more ways of keeping our thoughts active.

Believing and acting on this mentality that we are always "more" means that we are overwhelmed, left behind, nervous and irritated. Since we are still searching for "more," we unconsciously say to ourselves that what we recently have isn't enough, and we don't so subtly strengthen the flawed belief that we never are sufficient. Thus everything we do in our day-to-day lives (whether in the workforce or on the front of home) can be mired into exhaustion, drama, or rotten and tedious behaviour. Due to the fact that our lives are unconsciously determined to be lacking (why would we need "more" if we had enough?), our inner fire starts dwindling because of the lack of nutrition and fatigue. We never concentrate on the work in our heart, maybe because we forget or even do not know what kind of work makes our heart sings.

When we look at ourselves as artists instead of staff, homemakers, managers, or owners, we look beyond our small positions in the world. Our true job does not lie in the tasks we perform all day long but just outside them. We can only discover what our true job is when we look beyond them. And this is the secret to your artistic life. This relation to your true work and the fact that you see yourself as an artist fuels your inner fire.

My argument is that your true job is not really what you do, but, more importantly, how you do it and how you do it. In other words, the outer "work" you do – your tasks such as your workplace, career, jobs, and even parenting – is not your real job, but each of these items is a part of your preference or requirement.

Suffering and failure to fulfil result from the belief that the part you play is who you are. This is an error, and it is simple to produce. Just because you are a business accountant does not mean that your true job is accounting. "Accountant" is a role you've played in the world. You're doing something, not who you are. Suffering comes into the picture when you mistakenly call the accounting business your real job, as your inner peace is linked to any perceived success or failure in that position.

As you start thinking about what your actual job is and how you can embody it in all your activities let the following questions be thought out and write down your responses in a separate paper sheet:

- What's silence?

- What is faith?

- What is a cure?

- What's holy?

- What is thankfulness?

Do not try to answer the question immediately, but take a few moments and allow your answers to bubble from within.

These questions give us the opportunity to explore our relationship with our inner fire through these lenses as we move forward. If you take an inventory of what you are referring to now, you will have a baseline from which to start when we go through more exploration. It would also be fascinating to see if your responses to these questions are changing or expanding at the end of this book.

Your True Meaning Gifts.

- Your actual work isn't what you do; it's how you do it.

- Every day is an opportunity to connect to today's preciousness and start again in a sacred way. If we align our minds with our energies, emotions, and physical bodies, we harmonise with our inner wisdom.

Time	Activity	Energy Level	Feeling/ Experience
6:45 a.m.	woke up	low	sluggish
7 a.m.	breakfast	low	tired
7:15 a.m.	checked email	medium	overwhelmed
7:30 a.m.	drive to work	medium	lots of negative thoughts
7:45 a.m.	turned on music	high	better, more enthusiasm
8 a.m.	post office	medium	productive
8:15 a.m.	radio news	low	totally dampened my energy
8:30 a.m.	early to work	high	happy to have a half hour of quiet!
9 a.m.	phone calls	high	productive
9:15 a.m.	phone calls	high	productive
9:30 a.m.	meeting	low	really self-judgmental

Chapter 4
Find Your Faith

Agreements that come from fear need a lot of energy, but contracts from love allow us to conserve energy and even obtain additional energy.
"From Miguel Ruiz"

Although there are many facets of spirituality that concern your inner fire, one that I have found very useful is confidence in rising electricity. I know that faith always comes with baggage in today's culture. For some of us, faith is still a positive weapon, while for others; it has a number of negative connotations. We all know that some religious groups have used faith as a tool and that some of our science communities consider it childish nonsense.

So before we go any further, I would like to ask you to disregard your current believing ideas, be they optimistic or pessimistic, because I would ask you to look at faith in different ways.

Webster's Dictionary describes faith as "complete trust or trust in someone or something." From this standpoint, the fact is that almost all of us have confidence and trust stuff or people every day. For example, we switch the light to the belief that the lights are activated. We dial a telephone number and trust our beloved will answer. We get up in the morning; the sun will rise with confidence.

In this case, it seems like we all have a connection with faith even though we do not recognise it as such. In that lesson, we will use faith as a powerful weapon to lift our inner fire when we relate to its most profound aspect consciously.

In contrast to the many things that we unintentionally place trust in every day, your deepest faith is a deliberate decision. This is where you can choose to interact. For me, I want to bind to what I consider to be power bigger, deeper, or broader than I do. This kind of faith does not include promoting hierarchy or shirking responsibility; it is the clear acknowledgement that the universe is more significant than I am and that it works to my advantage.

I prefer to look at something greater than my tightly centred daily selves when I communicate with my deepest faith, and I choose to believe that this force is engineering conditions for my ultimate good. Many of us can hardly believe that our team and orchestra activities have a greater power to get us to the highest good. If you resist this proposal, that's all right too. Your deepest faith must not be a divine presence; it can be as simple as faith that tomorrow, as it did today, the sun will rise. I invite you to temporarily resist in order to explore the bond between your deepest faith and the inner fire for the sake of expertise.

Next, for a moment, I want you to rest, breathe deeply, and ask yourself a simple question: "Where do I want today to put my deepest faith?" I mentioned a few examples below. See which of them resonate in your being, if any:

- I believe it all unfolds as it should.

- I have confidence that for my ultimate benefit, the universe is coordinating circumstances.

- I believe that in my life, I can find a way to conquer obstacles.

- I have confidence that my angels, ancestors, and spiritual guides watch over me.

- I have confidence in my heart's wisdom.

- I have confidence in God. I have faith in God.

- I have Mother Earth confidence.

- I have life trust.

As for me, even in the hardest moments of life, this is all that I can believe:

- I'm sure I'm going to regain my confidence.

Now, after you've addressed the question of where you want to experience putting faith, that's what makes it different from holding faith, just as culture has taught us. Faith is about faith for most people in our culture – it is just a mental practice. But the faith I speak of is more than a logical process; it also involves the feeling of your faith instead of only thinking of holding it in your mind. It is a scientific decision to guide the energy in your body, your internal fire, to bind to a force that is bigger than you.

I always claim that the mind does not have to "believe in" the faith to be successful because it has all manner of views, suspicions, and negative convictions about the faith. But when you feel your confidence, you bind it deeper and better. This is a difficult conception to explain in words since, in today's culture, the act of feeling in your faith is not something we have to say. But it is a mechanism that goes beyond your thought mind, moves through your body, and makes your body feel linked. That can be a difficult thing to master, but our breath and our imagination are two very helpful instruments we all have for our deepest faith. For example, breathe deeply and feel the support of everything you want to place your trust in (Mother Earth, God, the confidence that everything is going as it should, etc.), and when you breathe out, imagine that any doubt, fear, or concern about the future or remorse of the past is being deliberately released.

Try to sense your inner energies when you do this. It may give you a feeling of electricity or pitching in your chest or heart, it may feel like loosening your shoulders as you relax into your energy, or it may feel like something else. If you look deep, you will find a feeling present both in your physical body and in your mind. Whatever the case. That's how you know you're starting to feel. A mindful breath here will activate the nervous system and slow down all other processes, which will allow you to be more fully aware of the strength of your deepest faith and better.

If we are overwhelmed, exhausted, and anxious, we do not associate our inner fire with our profound faith. Instead, we put our trust in the tasks before us, in our to-do list, and in our positions in the world instead of in our true work. We place our trust in temporary things and try to regulate their behaviour. I suggest connecting every morning to your deepest faith. I do this right along with clearing my mind so that I can have a strong, quiet basis for my day and cultivate this link to my clear mind and profound faith regardless of my duties. As I feel exhausted, depressed, or desire to regulate things, it's especially helpful for me to do this exercise again for a few moments and to come back to my deepest belief.

Chapter 5

Use Your Emotions

As my suffering grew up, I soon realised that there were two ways I could respond to my situation—either to react bitterly or to transform suffering into a creative force. I decided to pursue the direction of the latter.
—Luther King Jr. Martin Luther.

In the West, we are always told to distinguish ourselves from our feelings and to overuse the logical mind to be "efficient" and "efficient". Emotions are seen as responsibilities that reduce our efficiency and hinder our work. Moreover, the difficult feelings that we don't like make us anxious. Isn't there an excuse to stop them?

We need to understand the connection between our inner energy and our emotions in our quest to awaken our inner fire. We all have seen this interplay of feelings and energy many times in our lives, but we are not always sure of this.

For example, why do we always feel so much better after a good cry, even energised? Similarly, an assault by belly-laughs can also pump us up and ready to go. In both cases, our renewed energy is due to the connection between emotional release and inner fire. I call this form of emotional release an example of emotional flow permission. Instead of making us feel our feelings too much, we repress them so that the flow of our emotions gets backed up as though it had a dam. It doesn't feel good to begin and can contribute to our overwhelming stress or anger. But if we permit our emotions to flow and experience them, including the negative ones, we unlock the emotional barrier, which also lights up our inner fire.

What happens to our inner fire when we dam our emotions? It raises the question. My feeling is that you know the answer already: we feel exhausted because we use it with stuffing and containing and transporting these heavy emotions instead of using this free-flowing capacity to further our true working. Over time, we can accumulate heavy emotions for a lifetime without fully understanding their effect on our inner fire.

Imagine wearing a huge backpack full of all the feelings you have gathered in your lives. Any of these, like when you said to yourself, "I don't want to feel it," you might consciously put in your backpack and drove down something. Others were introduced unintentionally, maybe because you didn't realise what you were feeling at the moment or just couldn't say the emotion correctly. You have been holding these emotions for many years, like when your father left your life when you were seven, or your refusal to throw tears when you were a classmate said that you were ugly as a child, or even the overwhelming love you had for your classmate in secondary school because it had never been necessary.

Those feelings are not gone, even though you do not frequently think about them. What I discovered was that in our everyday lives, they could be reactivated if new circumstances cause them, but we are sometimes unaware of the link.

For example, when she was a kid, I have a friend whose dad died suddenly. She doesn't know what to do with her many emotions at the moment, partially because she grew up in a family that didn't speak about or shares their feelings much. She now, as an adult with children of her own, found that she was beginning to cry uncontrollably as she watched kid movies where a parent dies (animated movies like Disney's Lion King or Finding Nemo). To see the link, you don't have to be Sigmund Freud. For nearly thirty years, she brought her emotions with her, but it was only when she sat with her own chill over to watch these films that she ignited that reaction within her. When we spoke about it, she realised that when her father died, she hadn't expressed much of her grief but had tried to be "solid" for her family. Through our research, together, she realised that she held on to her old belief that "being strong means not weeping or voicing feelings" and could deliberately rewrite it into a new belief that "I am strong when I express my feelings." If necessary, she would weep and realise that she was an acting ally, showing her strength and energy much better than attempting to reverse those emotions for another 30 years.

In a less apparent case, another student found that he always had a highly emotional reaction when he felt "accused" of something he did not do. (He also observed that he was inclined to view questions as charges.) He also felt like he needed to protect those he saw falsely convicted and would be very frustrated and furious about news reports that revoked people from prison following a previously incorrect sentence (as sometimes happens with DNA evidence).

He told me about how his parents misrepresented him as a child and were severely punished and humiliated for him during one of our meetings. Since he never thought that his thoughts were wrong and knew about them, he stuffed these emotions and wanted to forget that they had ever occurred. Initially, as an adult, he did not think that this incident had an effect on him but, as we returned and explored it in depth, he saw how these formerly trapped feelings had an influence on his current life.

Whilst looking at our formative years is a useful place to begin with all our old feelings, many of us have far newer examples of this kind of stuffing.

Freeing Your Emotions Creates An Intuition Space

What I have found is that there is an incredible connection between a flowing and intuitive, emotional body. This is one of the fabulous benefits of attending to your emotional body: you are not only more adaptable and more energised and powerful but are also more attuned to the tendencies of your instincts. If we waste our energy filling our feelings, we cannot use these emotions as a guide and instructor, which is the essence of intuition. This is why we always think, when we encounter our intuition, "I have a feeling about this." Your feelings are a crucial part of learning to step through acts linked to the wisdom of your inner knowledge.

In other words, you tap into magic as you switch from concern to your inherent emotional intelligence.

Here the word magic is used to express the manifestation of the unexpected or anything beyond the ability of the mind to understand: "It was just as magical!"

You were possibly intimate with magic as a child. As youngsters, we always have invisible 'magic' friends and, rather than limits, our curious, open minds see potential. A childlike sense of wonder improves magic, while a rigid, rational emphasis distinguishes us from magic.

I've seen this kind of magic many times in my life, but a recent example came as I worked on the book launch for The War Rior Goddess Way. I had an enormous list of people to call the book tour I did, and I didn't know where to start. As I looked at this list, I could immediately feel anxiety and overwhelmingly start to surface.

My rational mind jumped in and said, "It's time to buckle down! Start at the start and work through the list." I could feel the overwhelming weights and "not enough" grumbling: I'll have insufficient time, I'll have too many, I'm not sufficient. I found how, throughout my time at Berkeley, I reminded myself of my emotions. So I closed my eyes and focused so that my emotions could flow. When I opened my eyes and looked back at the list, one of the names came up against me, and I felt a deep knowledge of my being.

Now call Kathy.

I opened my eyes and saw the clock. Kathy was the magazine editor in which I needed the article, and our time zones were such that Kathy was only 7 a.m.

"Now I can't call Kathy; it's too early!" my logistical mind replied.

Now the knowledge has come back from a place of peace, quiet presence, call Kathy.

"This is 7 a.m. You shouldn't call people before 9 a.m.," contradicted my mind.

Now call Kathy. Now call Kathy.

My rational mind was strongly opposed, for if I did what my emotional body told me to do, I feared Kathy would believe me to be rude. I had been trying to meet Kathy for a full month without success. The perfectionist who wanted to start with is at the top of the list and work in alphabetical order was also at this suggestion. My emotional body, however, kept telling me to function in this sense of constant awareness. I got the phone and called Kathy. I called Kathy.

To my reasonable surprise, Kathy answered the phone, was happy to hear from me, and we agreed to produce a paper and an event within five minutes. My inner self knew it was the force of intuition at work.

Listening to your emotionally cleared body's nudges and insights, which is your link to magic, to find ease and flow in your life.

Your True Work And Emotions

They can become a wonderful tool to find and keep in touch with your true work when you release your emotion. If something simply "feels right," in spite of what the rational mind can tell, it is bigger and more important wisdom than thinking alone.

Turning to our emotions will stimulate the fires of our inner fire by showing us what really matters.

Let's assume, for example, that you are in a position to choose between two jobs or career paths. Your rational brain can tell you to "take your high-paid work more securely and with more long-term growth potential," but your feelings make you feel well on the inside. Recently, a friend asked me what made me feel completely plentiful in my life. I began to think about the "usual" things most of us are trying to do: a home, a new car, and/or more money at the bank.

They felt nice to imagine, but I felt intuitive that there was more. I calmed down and again wondered, "What will make you feel abundant?" And the reply came as a feeling immediately: I would feel plentiful if I dedicated more time to a non-profit organisation that returned to others. My physical body settled down, and my emotional body was dancing happily because my heart and my true work were aligned and not my head's purely rational thoughts.

Aligning our emotional body with our true work has wonderful results, but the trick is to remain open to response without forcing one's standards of what you believe or want to be the answer. A friend of mine, for example, truly decided to leave her government job to become a massage therapist. She thought the service was her true work. But she was frightened and overwhelmed when she thought about leaving her job. At first, she assessed herself for her fear of leaping into a new area of profession. She decided she needed her feelings to drive herself.

We spoke for a while about this decision, and like us, I asked her, "What does your emotional body need to concentrate on your true work?"

Her immediate response was, "Stability".

"Great. Do you feel stable right now to leave your job?"

"No," she said to me. "But don't I have to struggle for my real work? Will I not let myself down if I stay in my work today?"

I urged her, "Listen to your body and emotions." "Here, what's true?"

When she let go of her thoughts and decided to feel her feelings, she reconnected to a sense of calm. "I have to first serve myself," she said, "and come to a point where I feel more comfortable and confident in myself and have more money on my savings account so that when I move into my real work, I can support myself. My work today is great for that. So I am doing my true work by staying in my job for now!"

It wasn't the answer she thought she would get, but note that there are no "correct" responses to life's many questions. The only real answers stem from an affectionate alliance with your emotional body and true work.

When we open our emotional bodies and permit healing the flow of magic, our inner fires burn even brighter. The end line is emotions – self is a form of energy, and when we damage it, we trap these emotions in us, where they havoc our inner fire's primal energy.

Emotional Cure

Here are a few things to flow your emotional energy. Take the list of feelings you have made in this lesson earlier and release some of the technicians below.

Talk out loud.

Look in a mirror, speak to yourself in the car, walk around, and tell what you want to let go by speaking loudly. Treat yourself to talking to the others concerned, if necessary, or address the forms in which you have kept yourself. Put an effort to use your words to let go of ways you are not true to yourself and adopt emotional integrity internally and externally.

Sing.

Crank your car's radio or download your favourite high school songs. Put your headphones on and stroll through nature. Belt it out! Belt it out! Practice singing as loudly as possible to clear blocks of expression. Have fun! Have fun!

Make sounds of animals.

This is an unorthodox way of moving old or trapped feelings, but it works, really. Think of a word of feeling you wrote and make a sound that you know is the same. For instance, when you're angry, hurt, embarrassed, or guilty, try to groan, grunt and cry. Exaggerate, open your mouth wide, and let the animal out! Try other emotions about other sounds. There is no wrong way of doing that.

Exercise the feelings.

Go for a long walk and render facial gestures that are exaggerated as you feel and show various emotions. Squeeze your face up and raise your arms in the air as you feel rage. Open your mouth with ecstasy. Let your face and body shift the feeling of a broken heart. What does fear sound when it's blown into big gestures? Let your body and face prove it. What about love? What about love? Jealousy? Is there any frustration? Excitingly? Maintain the gestures and expressions between various emotional conditions. It will at first feel uncomfortable, but stick to it, and you will soon find that the language of your emotions will be more fluent.

Be imaginative.

It takes a creative spirit to unlock trapped or stuck emotions and knock down the old barrier, which overflows the river of your emotions. Open yourself to colourful ways to unload the old bag.

- **Such imaginative ways of moving anger:** Find a safe spot for old plates to break. (We will cover our eyes and take other appropriate safety measures!) Glass break in a recycling bin. (As above, make sure you first put your safety.)

- **Fill with water and freeze paper milk cartons.** Throw them down on the sidewalk! Throw them down! It is super satisfactory to break the ice on concrete and then to melt.

- Chop wood (with this one super-mindful and safe!). Tear up phone books. Phonebooks.

Such imaginative ways of moving grief:

- See a sad film and let the sensations flow. Give yourself the chance to weep.

- Get a blanket, curl tightly up, and rock side by side your body.

- Write down what you miss/long for before the tears arrive.

Support Your Temple

Explore the individual needs with simple body treatment. What are you eating? What are you eating? What's your body pulling down? What does your body actually nourish? Patience: it sometimes takes some time to wire around the body because our customs are deeply engraved, particularly when it comes to using food not as a clean fuel to regenerate and feed our cells but as just a fast fix to keep our body going. We will use whatever we need in this latter mentality, be it excess caffeine or sugar or whatever.

These two are the worst for the body. If you know your physical body has unhealthy habits, be gentle again with yourself and start listing the habits that you would like to alter at a time. Choose one area to concentrate on. If you have something you can't manage – you have a newborn, so sleep is unpredictable – be imaginative with your ideas or focus on feeding yourself in other places.

Upgrading one thing at a time will support the body. This week you don't have to do everything –take just one habit and keep yourself steady. If you hit a block, let your body, not your mind, answer the question. If you have developed a new routine or re-established the patterns of your body, the next thing on your list can be approached with a sense of facility and presence.

Here are some practical measures to feed your body in a new way. These exercises will help you learn about yourself and your true physical requirements. They even have morsel sizes, which I find very helpful. Instead, say to yourself: "I'll just eat food my body likes and sleep for the rest of my life eight hours a day," say to myself: "Let me conduct this experiment the next week as a way to help and think about my body." Taking a practice in your mind as an experiment with a beginning, a centre, and an end will give you a greater focus and help you succeed.

You may want to join a gym or wellness club for additional assistance or maybe ask a friend to join you on a journey of honour. You don't have to do it alone. Be imaginative again!

Sleep.

Plan a week when you can sleep for at least 8 hours a night. Make sure that you're ready! Don't schedule ahead for the week late nights. Remove your phone, turn off your TV an hour before bed, and make your morning routine easy for you. Remember how the body feels at the end of the week.

Food.

Choose one thing from your diet that you want to remove (start with only one thing you want to improve, then add more the following week!). Again, do some preparation in advance. For instance, if you cut out sugar, ensure that you have apples or other low-sugar dishes in your house and bring alternate-tive snacks to you. If you are eating milk, see what you can do to replace it. Know that the first few days will be awkward, and remain consistent with yourself.

Exercise.

Our bodies love and need exercise, especially as we grow older or spend a lot of time in front of the computer. If you don't exercise right now, start tiny. Commit to moving every other day for one week, for at least five minutes to an hour. Take a quick stroll, swim, dance to music, pump iron, run, do yoga—you have to try so much. See how you feel at the end of the week. Repeat. Repeat.

Touch.

I believe most of us are hungry for contact; the present, caring touch is needed in our bodies. Begin by putting your heart and hand on your belly and saying hi. Pay attention when you take a shower or a bath to offer your present touch when washing your body. Hug people. Cuddle your pets or mates. Cuddle up.

Physical treatment.

Do you have any ways to stop simple body maintenance? I am talking about stuff like good teeth hygiene, a lot of water to drink, and checking with a doctor – whatever self-care is best for you. Choose one thing that you have avoided, and take action this week.

You will start to nourish and honour your body with stressful sittings by trying these small measures. Finally, the physical response to stress will change, allowing even in times of crisis to respond calmly and centrally. Keep asking your body for help and guidance, and it will come. Let the wisdom of your body come out.

The Technique Of Pomodoro

If you have to work for long hours sitting or standing, take daily breaks, even if they are few. If you work on your computer or if you're in a similar focus, I suggest the body-friendly procedure, which has an app, which I use when I write.

Francesco Cirillo developed the Pomodoro technique, which is super quick. You use a timer to build concentration periods followed by brief rest periods. The technique of Pomodoro breaks down like this:

Round	Task	Timer
1	Work/Focus	25 minutes
	Rest/Break	5 minutes
2	Work/Focus	25 minutes
	Rest/Break	5 minutes
3	Work/Focus	25 minutes
	Rest/Break	5 minutes
4	Work/Focus	25 minutes
	Long Rest/Break	15–30 minutes

You first work for 25 minutes and then take a 5-minute break. This stage is repeated three times (or three "rounds"). On the fourth round, you work 25 minutes, then take a longer break, normally between 15 and 30 minutes.

I love this way because 25 minutes are enough to flow, but not so long that my body gets too sluggish. And five minutes is enough time to stretch, drink water, jump jackets, or make a cup of tea without losing my thread.

I started squats, jumping ropes, and literally running around the block during my lunch. I find this approach doubly advantageous as I do more work but still remain linked to my body's wisdom.

Chapter 6

Gratitude: The Igniter Energy

Gratitude is the secret to joy and equanimity, not
comprehension.
—Anne Lamott.

Have you ever heard of Mystical Fire powder? It is available in a rectangular plastic black package with rainbow letters. To use the torch, you gain a powerful blazing campfire and sprinkle a bit of Mystical Fire powder, and boom – the familiar orange flames become a rainbow of colours. Dance before your eyes green, blue, and purple fire.

To burn your inner fire with gratitude is to add rainbows to your flames of a campfire: everything becomes richer and more beautiful. Having an attitude of appreciation enables us to view our lives as a valuable, unique gem, which is our blessed lifetime to carve and polish. Like an artist, we can make this gem shine with rich colours by focussing on our true work every day, and gratitude is a tool that makes our gem shine. It is not surprising that the few people who are identified as "illuminated" always agree that their lives are a continuous state of gratitude.

For the rest of us, appreciation comes easily, and our inner fire burns brightly when we're in a good position. It is as though you gladly threw delicious sweet oil on your inner feast and a bucket of mystic fire powder. You are so vividly lit up by the fragrance of the perfume and the richness of the colours that your inspired glass extends to all around you.

If things don't go well, this appreciation is usually even more difficult to find. When students or friends come to me in the midst of a tough life sitting around and finding it hard to connect with gratitude (or some sense of hope), I give them a simple assignment: write down five items every day, for which you are thankful.

These five items can be small: I'm thankful for inhaling this. I'm thankful that I'm sitting on this chair. I'm thankful both of my weapons work. I am glad that in my bank account I have five dollars. I'm grateful for my dog's warm brown eyes to look at me.

In our hardest moments, we may not be thankful even for these names, but if we are able to turn our attention to the things that we are thankful for, we nourish our inner fire and work towards healing ourselves and the world around us.

And the weakest flame improves with a constant application of gratitude. When the inner fire becomes more radiant, as we reminisce of our true work and hear the silent wisdom in us, we will reveal everything we need to put our fire back on a safe burn.

In this way, thankfulness is a type of exercise, and if you do it consistently, the muscle of thanksgivings gets stronger over time. Thanksgiving is like heart push-ups and yoga for the mind:

It nourishes and raises the spirit. As we mentioned beforehand, connecting physically with gratitude is an excellent way of building the muscle of gratitude. Again, it's a matter of being grateful, much like feeling in faith, to discover what gratitude feels in your body and to use this physical experience to anchor your emotion. Just as we did in this book about faith before, let us remove the word "gratitude" from an idea or belief and make it feel.

This is a quick exercise so that you can feel what I say.

First of all, think of something for which you are thankful, big or small, miraculous or worldly. Is it something that took you recently to the tears of joy or a recollection of 40 years ago, that your baby smiled over you yesterday or that spectacular moonrise over the mountains when you camped as a child? Bring all your senses and sharpen your memory's concentration. Breathe in, fill up, and feel in each cell.

Now let go of the memory that triggered gratitude and only concentrates on the sense of gratitude that your body gives. Where do you feel gratitude? How do you feel in your chest? How does your stomach feel? Does it tingle your skin? Next, remember what your inner fire feels like. Then inhale, exhale. Be grateful and imagine with every breath that you will make your body feel more and more.

One thing you know when you feel in your gratuitousness is that it's not really what is outside of you that causes these wonderful feelings (although they can induce them). Any occurrence outside of you can be a catalyst for appreciation, but the emotion itself comes from inside you rather than from outside the world. We can say thanks can be an option in this way.

I want to share a story I have found on the Internet that quite clearly expresses this concept. It's one of these stories nobody knows from where it originated, or whether it's true or not, but regardless, the message is 100% true and something we must all take to heart.

STORY

The 92-year-old, tiny, comfortable, proud lady today moved to a nursing home. Her 70-year-old band recently passed away, making it necessary to travel. When the nurse said that her room was ready, she smiled sweetly after several hours of patiently waiting in the lobby of his nursing home. The nurse identified her tiny room and pointed out all the things she noticed when she got there, including the eyelet rings on her mirror, as she manoeuvred her walker to the lift. With a new puppy newly introduced to an eight-year-old, she exclaimed, "I love it," before the lift had even reached her floor.

"Mrs. Jones, you have not seen the bed." The nurse said that.

"It has nothing to do with it," answered Ms. Jones. "Happiness is something that you know in advance. Whether I like my room or not depends on how the furnishings are arranged; I organise my mind.

I decided to love it already. It's a decision I make when I wake up every morning. I have a choice: I can stay in bed all day, moaning about the parts of my body that don't function, or I can get up and be grateful for the ones that do."

Like the heroine in this story, you too can choose how you see the world and how you organise things. As we explored earlier, our responses to these conditions, which have an effect on our well-being, are not what happens the world over. This is also true of appreciation. Wherever we focus our attention – whether on pain or on gratitude – that's what will develop in my experience.

When you pull the strong threads of indignation, blame, disgrace, or loss through your being's cloth, you continue to weave those qualities into everything you see, think, do. When you lovingly recognise the difficulties and hurts of the past as you search for the ever-present threads of miracles and moments of love, you are weaving deep golden lines of appreciation in what you see, think and do.

Take some time to relax the next time you're stressed, overwhelmed, or in pain, and ask yourself this easy question: "What do I thank you for right now?" When you find that, replay it again and again in your head. Stay present and note if your inner energy starts shifting from pain to surrender, even if it's a slight change. Allowing you to note even the slightest change is an indication that it's all right to unwind. This is the first step to release your suffering by focusing your awareness on gratitude.

I know firsthand that life can be hard; please understood. Loved ones are dying. Finance is crumbling. Problems of health occur. Relationships are over. It's at these times that we have to be remarkably brave enough to choose to concentrate on gratitude rather than negativity. Be gentle with yourself and note that gratefulness and sorrow can be experienced at once; this is the complexity and beauty of humanity.

Chapter 7

Fire Explorations Inside

The Royal Review

I want to share something I do with you on a large basis that I call the "Royal Review". Many spiritual practices recommend a daily examination of the components of your life, but I have noticed that your review from a peaceful, ventilated, freely versatile, grateful position is extremely necessary. It makes you remember that you rightly wear the courts of knowledge and relation in your life. This is what the Royal Review is about. You will see a wider image of what is right for you and your inner fire from a place of appreciation.

Although other spiritual beliefs and self-help activities promote a daily inventory, people frequently do this from an area of shortage, concentrating on what is wrong instead of being grateful for it all.

As a ruler with your own destiny, you take responsibility and leadership in the wellbeing and abundance of your entire realm. As a wise king, your subjects – the mental, the moral, the emotional, and physical parts of yourself – are carefully listened to, and your general wellbeing is kept in mind. You know and respect the duty and can see imbalances when they occur and fix them until they impact the whole kingdom from this overall viewpoint.

As your own queen or king, your tasks include the awareness of the thoughts which emerge in your mental landscape and the choice between honesty and liberation. You watch what happens in your emotional realm and make sure your emotions are more shared than discarded. In your spiritual world, you try to remain rooted in your religion instead of being blown by the winds of occupation and a need to rule. You respect the needs of the physical realm; you honour your body as the vehicle you view the world and take all appropriate measures to help it.

You examine all your domains from a position of thankfulness and humility because you know that with these unique forces, you are fortunate enough to be here with the best rulers who are wrong.

So at the end of every day, as the ruler of your own inner kingdom, I invite you to ask your "subjects" the following questions and listen to the reports which return regarding the state of your concern with an open heart:

Mental Realm.

What parts of you wore the crown today in your men's realm? What was your time consumed by thinking and your energy drained? Who fed your energy? When did you have insight moments?

Emotional Kingdom.

What feelings have you had, and what has caused them today? Have you allowed them to flow? If not, what does it want to express?

Spiritual Realm.

What steps have you taken to cultivate a spiritual ally? Have you been founded on your true faith? Or did you have times when you were overwhelmed with fear and worry? Have you tried to regulate situations instead of flowing?

Physical Realm.

How have you today treated your body? Have you heard it and given it what it needs? Or maybe you missed it and forgot about it?

Remember, when you answer these questions every day at the top, from a place of appreciation, you will always do so. Take your responses to "I should be" – like "I should have listened more to my body," "I will not try to manipulate situations" –because it isn't a place to beat up (and to be clear, no place is good for that). This exercise is intended to understand from what your analysis reveals, appreciate the steps you made, to gain more insight from your whole being on what fuels your inner fire and what drains it so that the next time you choose it better.

And, when you do this because you are rooted in a position of thankfulness, you will be imaginative and concentrate your true work on all aspects of your life.

Chapter 8

The Internal Fire Prayer: A Daily Practice To Get It Together

Wonderful, incredible things come to us.

Lives when we pay care: mangoes, grandsons, Bach, ponds. This occurs most often when we have the lowest possible expectations. You're in trouble if you say, "Well, that's pretty much what I'd think I'd see." You must ask yourself at that point why you're here. In our lives, astonishing material and revelation emerge all the time. Let it be. Let it be. So much is entrusted to us. We just need to be available to the company.

—Anne Lamott.

Throughout this book, we have studied four facets of ourselves – mental, spiritual, emotive, and physical – and how each of them relates to our internal fire.

Of these four aspects, I clarified how, particularly when it comes to interacting with the outside world, we rely most heavily on our mental processes or thought. I trust it is sensible to accept that we overthink things as opposed to building up all things reasonably on the grounds that our way of life has given a higher need to our idea.

The problem with this approach is that we are disconnecting from the other realms when we depend too heavily on one part of ourselves.

This also results in us neglecting our physical bodies, repressing our emotions, and/or ignoring the inner direction of our spiritual existence at a considerable cost to our total wellbeing.

We must learn to use the power of our own mind, along with the deep knowledge of our body, our emotions, and our spirituality, to carry out our true work through these four interrelated facets of our being to bring about equilibrium and peace into our day. We fan the flames of our inner fire through the integration of these four elements, resulting in a very linked and gratifying existence.

I wrote a powerful prayer (or mantra, if you prefer) to help incorporate all the teachings in this book; that is, I call the Inner Fire Prayer a way to equal all facets of ourselves. Through our everyday practice, which involves a prayer/mantra, we use the power of the mind and the words (since our word forms in mind) to attract attention to the other aspects. In some way, we might suggest that we use the power of the mind to travel beyond the mind itself and to draw attention equal to all facets of ourselves.

I originally developed the Internal Fire Prayer for myself as a new way of opening up my true work process, and in my daily life, I started to use it. Soon after that, I discovered that it began to work through me when I began to consistently use the Inner Fire Prize. When I get stressed or busy, the words of the prayer gladly appear to me, like a sweet angel at the door that reminds me to be linked to all facets of myself and put my true work into the present everyday tasks. Here is the prayer which sums up all we learned in this book:

The Fire Internal Prayer

Can I clear my mind of all thoughts and concentrate on silence?

Can I clear up my area of operation and communicate with my deepest faith?

May I open my emotional body and allow the flow of healing?

May I respect this physical shape as a sacred temple?

Can I go with an appreciation for this precious time for my highest reason?

Golden Self Love Journal

Everyday Questions You Should Ask Yourself For 3 Weeks

First Week

Acceptance Journal Prompts.

I am a firm believer that self-love journaling must constantly embark on with approval. In case you don't know where to start on your way to cherishing yourself, start here.

1. What are simply the five things that I really acknowledge?

   ....

   ....

   ....

   ....

   ....

2. What part of myself do I wish to improve the most?

....

....

....

....

....

3. How do I first hug and appreciate that part of myself?

....

....

....

....

....

4. Where am I permitting myself to be little?

....

....

....

....

....

5. Do I allow myself to acknowledge praises from others?

....
....
....
....
....

6. What part of myself do I track down the hardest to cherish?

....
....
....
....
....

7. What would it be a good idea for me to do to begin adoring that part of myself?

....
....
....
....
....

Second Week

Self-Worth and Confidence Journal Prompts.

Remember these inquiries for your scratch pad to help you rest easy thinking about yourself, your body, your brain, and your propensities.

1. What parts of myself do I appreciate?

   ....

   ....

   ....

   ....

   ....

2. What do I believe myself to be pleased with?

   ....

   ....

   ....

   ....

   ....

3. Make a rundown of the five things you despise about yourself. How might I reshape them into a restricting conviction? For instance: I scorn my thighs yet love them since they permit me to walk.

....
....
....
....
....

4. What are my abilities?

....
....
....
....
....

5. What are my most noteworthy desires?

....
....
....
....
....

6. What recognises me?

....

....

....

....

....

7. How might I utilise my singularity in my day-by-day life?

....

....

....

....

....

8. What is something I wish any other individual would advise me?

....

....

....

....

....

9. How do I help myself to remember this all the more as often as possible?

....

....

....

....

....

10. What do I think I am qualified for?

....

....

....

....

....

11. What makes me believe I'm deserving of it?

....

....

....

....

....

12. What is it that I am especially talented at?

....

....

....

....

....

13. What garments do I like wearing and cause me to feel great in?

....

....

....

....

....

14. What are five qualities of my current self that my previous self would appreciate?

....

....

....

....

....

15. What parts of my character do I respect?

....

....

....

....

....

16. What do I like about my body?

....

....

....

....

....

Third Week

Self-Love Journal Prompts.

Please get back to these confidence diaries prompts as much as important; a few of these philosophical inquiries expect us to address them at different periods or phases of our lives so that the appropriate responses will change!

1. What would I do if I cherished myself today?

    ....

    ....

    ....

    ....

    ....

2. How am I going to help myself today?

    ....

    ....

    ....

    ....

    ....

3. What brings me delight?

....

....

....

....

....

4. What does somebody who loves themselves get done for themselves?

....

....

....

....

....

5. What gives me a feeling of aliveness?

....

....

....

....

....

6. What limits do I set for myself?

....

....

....

....

....

7. What am I doing that holds me back from being with myself?

....

....

....

....

....

8. What would I do each day if I adored myself?

....

....

....

....

....

9. What is an everyday guarantee I should make to myself to cherish myself?

....

....

....

....

....

10. To whom may I show more love? (At the point when you offer more love, you will get more love from yourself as well as other people.)

....

....

....

....

....

11. How could my optimal day look?

....

....

....

....

....

12. How do I deal with individuals I care about?

....
....
....
....
....

13. How would I be able to do likewise for myself?

....
....
....
....
....

14. Who propels me?

....
....
....
....
....

15. What is it about them that I find so engaging?

....

....

....

....

....

16. What did I appreciate doing as a kid?

....

....

....

....

....

I trust you tracked down these self-esteem journaling prompts educational and accommodating in getting more mindful. On the off chance that your confidence venture is simply starting, congrats; it is a once in a blue moon experience.

SCAN QR CODE AND GET AUDIO BOOK

FOR FREE!

To my dear readers,

We are thankful that you decided to buy this book. As special gift we can offer you the audio book for free. Just scan the QR code and download for free on Audible:

Please scan with your mobile phone:

*Just possible for new Audible customers.

Disclaimer

This book contains opinions and ideas of the author and is meant to teach the reader informative and helpful knowledge while due care should be taken by the user in the application of the information provided. The instructions and strategies are possibly not right for every reader and there is no guarantee that they work for everyone. Using this book and implementing the information/recipes therein contained is explicitly your own responsibility and risk. This work with all its contents, does not guarantee correctness, completion, quality or correctness of the provided information. Misinformation or misprints cannot be completely eliminated.

Printed in Great Britain
by Amazon

83037325R00064